Original title:
The Room with a View

Copyright © 2025 Creative Arts Management OÜ
All rights reserved.

Author: Miriam Kensington
ISBN HARDBACK: 978-1-80587-044-9
ISBN PAPERBACK: 978-1-80587-514-7

Panorama of Dreams

A window wide, I see the street,
Where neighbors dance, and pigeons greet.
A cat takes aim at a passing bee,
While I sip coffee, feeling free.

The mailman slips, a comic sight,
His packages soar, a postman's flight.
I chuckle softly, oh what a scene,
In this daily play, I'm the unseen.

Gaze Beyond the Glass

The neighbors bicker, what a mess,
Their loud debates are pure excess.
I can't help but laugh at their wild claims,
While I throw popcorn at their games.

A dog in a hat trots past my door,
I blink in shock, then laugh some more.
Life through glass is a vibrant play,
Where surreal meets the everyday.

Horizons Unfolding

A child with crayons draws the sky,
While parents wonder, 'Oh my, oh my!'
Loud laughter echoes from the park,
As squirrels practice their acorn arc.

Blinds drawn tight can't hide the fun,
Each peek outside reveals a run.
With humor bright and spirits high,
I join their joy without a sigh.

Echoes of the Outside

A bicycle zooms, a child goes 'Whee!'
My heart races fast with pure glee.
The ice cream truck comes, a jolly sound,
As kids chase dreams that swirl around.

A man in a cape, a superhero bold,
Mistaken for fame, or just plain old?
With one wink, he saves the day,
While I sit back, content to stay.

The Window's Silent Serenade

In the corner sits a chair,
Dust bunnies dance without a care.
The drapes whisper secrets soft,
While cats plot schemes from aloft.

A squirrel taps like it's a knock,
To share tales of the ticking clock.
Birds sing jingles from trees so high,
While I ponder why squirrels won't fly.

A Portrait of Possibility

Outside a canvas, alive and bright,
Painting stories in morning light.
The neighbors argue from dawn till noon,
While I sip coffee, just like a cartoon.

The sunbeams tickle my nose and chin,
While pigeons gossip on a whim.
Oh, what a show through this glass frame,
Life's a circus, but who's to blame?

Views That Envelop the Heart

Trees wave hello, oh what a sight,
As cars zoom by without a fright.
A dog in a tutu prances with glee,
While I chuckle, savoring my tea.

People traipse by, all in a rush,
Nature holds still, in a gentle hush.
With every glance, I laugh and smile,
The world puts on a show worthwhile.

Light Leaks and Shadow Play

Sunlight spills, a soft embrace,
As shadows stretch, they dance and race.
I peek through blinds, a secret spy,
At the silly antics of passersby.

Beneath the sunlight, colors bloom,
As kids concoct chaos in each room.
The laughter echoes, a joyful tune,
In this house made of laughs, bathed in maroon.

Sightlines of Serenity

Through the glass, a cat sprawls wide,
Chasing dreams, with tails as guides.
Birds perform their aerial ballet,
While I sip coffee, life's grand buffet.

Sunlight dances on the floor,
As socks twirl and the dust bunnies soar.
The world outside, all hustle and fuss,
But here, my heart beats in soft, joyful trust.

Quiet Corners for Contemplation

In a chair that creaks like old tales,
I ponder life through a sea of snails.
The fridge hums tunes of great delight,
While my snack stash awaits the night.

A moth flutters, trying to impress,
Just like me in a lovely dress.
Outside, the neighbors loudly argue,
I just chuckle, peeking askew.

A Vista for the Wanderer

Through the glass, the world unfolds,
A parade of people, young and old.
A dog steals lunch from a passerby,
While I munch popcorn, oh my, oh my!

The postman slips on a banana peel,
As I gasp and struggle to conceal.
From my perch of safety, I can see,
Life's grand spectacle, pure comedy!

Through the Transparent Barrier

I watch the world with intrigued eyes,
As neighbors practice their surprise pies.
Laughter erupts, then silence quakes,
A cupcake fight? Oh, for goodness' sakes!

The sun sets low, hues melt and blend,
As chuckles linger, we pretend.
Outside, the chaos and cheer collide,
I smile, for this joy I can't abide.

Daylight Revelations

Sunlight dances on the floor,
Dust bunnies become folklore.
The chair squeaks like a comedy,
Wonders of the day, so silly and free.

Birds audition on the sill,
With every chirp, they hope to thrill.
The cat plays judge, with skeptical eye,
As shadows leap and giggle by.

Silhouettes Against the Sky

In the window frame, I see the show,
Neighbors arguing over a gnome's glow.
A dog barks loud, it's a canine call,
While pigeons hold court, snappy and tall.

Clouds play hide and seek all day,
As if the sun forgot the way.
My coffee mug, a faithful friend,
Laughs at life; the humor won't end.

The Veil of Distance

Across the street, a man with flair,
Wears a hat that doesn't care.
His dance moves echo with every breeze,
While I sip tea and giggle with ease.

The squirrel spies from its lofty perch,
Judging styles, a furry church.
With leaps and bounds, it steals the scene,
Making my worries feel unseen.

Outside Voices Within

Neighbors chatter like a sitcom cast,
In every tale, a laugh is cast.
The gossip flies in rhythmic tones,
While my walls absorb the funny groans.

A child's laughter, pure and bold,
Turns mundane moments into gold.
As life unfolds from the window view,
I'm the audience, entertained anew.

Afterglow in the Daylight

Sunshine spills through the cracks,
A cat claims the window ledge.
Birds chirp gossip about snacks,
While I plot my next pledge.

Coffee stains on my old sheet,
A dance of air and drift.
Socks mismatched on my feet,
The sun gives my brain a lift.

A Tapestry Woven in Views

Pictures framed with random flair,
A rug that has seen better days.
Lampshades tilted in thin air,
Dust bunnies waltz in a haze.

Backyard chairs tell tales of woe,
While plants conspire with the breeze.
A squirrel's acrobatic show,
Turns ordinary life to tease.

Beyond the Mundane Scene

The toaster's bread performs a feat,
As butter slips with style and grace.
Outside, kids rollerblade on the street,
While I avoid life's fast-paced race.

Neighbors' laughter echoes bright,
As I peek through the curtain's veil.
Gossipy winds take flight,
In this accidental tale.

Fields of What-If

Mismatched curtains sway and sway,
Unruly plants climb ever high.
Imagined worlds drift lightly away,
As colors mingle in the sky.

A shoe left out, the joke runs deep,
What if it had legs of its own?
In this cozy, chaotic heap,
I ponder life's twisted tone.

Where the Sky Meets the Soul

A window wide, the sun peeks through,
The cat leaps high, all is askew.
Birds chirping 'bout their day so bright,
I sip my tea, what a silly sight.

The clouds parade, like cotton candy,
While squirrels dance, so wild and dandy.
My neighbor's hat flew past my nose,
Chasing thoughts, where laughter grows.

Fragments of Infinity

A glimpse of joy in every hue,
The popcorn machine buzzes anew.
I spy a joke in every cloud,
With laughter echoing, bold and loud.

The curtains flap, a playful tease,
The plants sway, they've caught a breeze.
With every glance, a chuckle found,
In this chaos, joy is crowned.

Beyond the Clear Barrier

Behind the glass, a world of cheer,
A dog barks loud, I nudge my beer.
The sunbeams dance on the floor,
This party's livelier than before.

A fly zooms by, a curious guest,
Bouncing 'round—oh, what a jest!
Laughter jumps from room to room,
As shadows play, dispelling gloom.

Embracing Distant Echoes

The distant laughter spills like wine,
A joke's replayed, it's divine!
The wind reports on gossip's chase,
While I sip slow, a smiling face.

The clock ticks loud, a ticklish tease,
As friends drop by with such sweet ease.
We share our thoughts, a splendid brew,
Life's just a joke, with friends so true.

Beyond the Sill

A cat on the windowsill, so grand,
Judges the world with a flick of its hand.
It flicks its tail, a regal decree,
As birds fly by, too blind to see.

The neighbor's dog gives a puzzled bark,
While squirrels plot mischief, the skies grow dark.
All this drama, a show from above,
In this tiny space, we see it all unfold with love.

Light Through the Lattice

Sunlight dances on my breakfast plate,
I swear it winked, oh what a fate!
Toast smiles back, a buttered grin,
These morning antics, where do I begin?

The jam jar jives, a fruity delight,
While coffee cups cheer with caffeine might.
A spectacle brewed, morning's own play,
Who knew breakfast could brighten the day?

Reflections on the Edge

Mirror, mirror, on the wall,
Who's the funniest of them all?
A blurry face looks back, oh dear,
I thought I'd brushed my hair—oh here!

The smudged lipstick tells its tale,
As I fish for dreams set to sail.
With every glance, a chuckle shared,
Who knew reflections could be so bared?

The Canvas of Daylight

In morning light, my socks collide,
One red, one blue—a fashion guide!
As sunlight spills on my mismatched feet,
I dance to a rhythm, oh what a treat!

The curtains sway like a brush in hand,
Creating art, unplanned, unplanned.
Each ray a color, bright and bold,
A masterpiece lives, or so I'm told.

Window to Whispers

Through the glass, gossip flows,
Neighbors chat while mischief grows.
A cat's tail flicks, a dog replies,
Laughter echoes through the skies.

Socks on lines are quite the sight,
Flinging tales from morning light.
Who knew laundry had a voice?
In a fabric world, we rejoice.

Birds perched up like spies on fun,
Count the stories one by one.
With every peek, a tale unfolds,
Such secrets traded, time retold.

Oh, the drama seen each day,
From silly pranks to love's ballet.
In this frame, the world so wide,
It's a comedy we can't hide.

Sunlight Through Shutters

Sneaky rays invade my space,
Dancing wildly, setting pace.
Sunshine tickles, shadows play,
Mischief found in light's ballet.

A floating dust mote's grand parade,
Performing tricks, they won't evade.
They swirl up high, dip down low,
Caught in beams, they steal the show.

With sleepy yawns, the world awakes,
Coffee brews and laughter quakes.
Who needs alarms with such a scene?
Sunshine spills the joy unseen.

Shutters creak, a playful sound,
Morning mischief all around.
Each new beam a joke unfolds,
In this bright room, life extols.

Framed Eternity

Pictures hung, a lovely mess,
Each frame holds laughs, a sweet excess.
A winking friend, a dancing pet,
Moments caught we can't forget.

Uncle Bob's face in a cake,
A gift from fate, a silly mistake.
His frosting crown, a regal sight,
Captured joy in pure delight.

Grandma's smile from years gone by,
A tender grin, a heartfelt sigh.
In each snapshot, stories dwell,
A scripted life, we know too well.

Time moves on but laughs remain,
In this gallery, joy's refrain.
From silly poses to heartfelt cheer,
Each frame whispers, "Stick around here!"

The Art of Longing

Peering out, I dream the day,
What's beyond in bright array?
A curious world, it calls my name,
Yet here I sit, it's all a game.

Pigeons coo as if they know,
Their world apart, the seeds they sow.
While I sip tea, they strut and tease,
Perhaps I'll join, if just to please.

The baker's truck grows ever near,
A scent of croissants tickles the air.
But still I linger, caught in thought,
My heart's desire, yet not sought.

They laugh and play, the children shout,
Outside my glass, life twirls about.
Oh, artful longing, sweet and sly,
From this perch, I'll wave goodbye.

Imagined Journeys from Glass

At the window I sit and stare,
A world outside that seems quite rare.
With every glance, adventures bloom,
In fantasies, I sweep the gloom.

A cow wears glasses, how absurd!
It plays the piano, quite the word!
Trains ride on puffed clouds of cream,
While I sip tea and further dream.

A cat in a hat spins tales so bright,
Of moonlit dances and stars at night.
Fluffy bunnies drift in the breeze,
I'll join them soon, just pass the cheese!

The view is chaos, a funny sight,
My imagination takes its flight.
A world of whimsy from my seat,
In glass-bound realms, life can't be beat.

Conversations with the Clouds

I chat with clouds, they're quite a crowd,
One says he's wise, and really loud.
He tells me jokes, like 'Why the rain?'
'To water plants, but I can't explain!'

The cumulus chuckles, the stratus sighs,
They gossip of storms and sunny skies.
They trade their tales of drifting dreams,
While I munch popcorn and sip my creams.

"Have you met a rainbow?" one cloud asks me,
"He's flashy, but also quite the Glee."
I nod in laughter, we all agree,
These airy pals bring glee for free!

Their fluffy forms change each minute,
Balloons or animals, they're never in it.
Conversations whirl, we float and dip,
With clouds as pals, I never trip!

Chains of Thought Untethered

My mind's a kite that's caught the breeze,
It dances high with grace and ease.
Thoughts flap like flags, both bright and bold,
Each one a story waiting to be told.

Why did the chicken cross the line?
To get some laughs, and maybe shine!
Ideas bounce like balls in the air,
A circus performance with flair to spare.

A chain of thoughts, not bound by weight,
They zip and zoom, oh, aren't they great?
A slice of pizza gives me a thought,
'Is a triangle a slice or just caught?'

With every twist, my laughter grows,
Untethered thoughts, in joy they flow.
A merry dance in the mind's wide space,
Creating delight at a funny pace!

The Whispering Wind Beneath

The wind, she whispers sweet secrets low,
Of ticklish trees and dancing flow.
She carries tales on a feathery wing,
Of spaghetti clouds and a moonlit fling.

"She tickles feathers, makes them fly,"
Said the bird, flapping with a sigh.
"Why do we sing? It's just for fun,
To chase away clouds, a job well done!"

Below, the flowers chuckle and sway,
As gusts of giggles come out to play.
Each rustling leaf shares a joke or two,
About a frog who liked the hue!

With breezy laughter, their chatter's free,
Whispers of joy, oh, what glee!
The world spins round, a merry spin,
Echoes of joy with the wind's soft grin.

Gaze into the Infinite

I peek through the glass, oh what a sight,
The neighbor's cat has taken flight.
With feathered friends out on a spree,
Chasing shadows, just like me.

A dog in shades, he struts with flair,
Who knew canines would fashion dare?
The world outside, a circus show,
While I just sip my morning Joe.

A kid on a bike, he wobbles wild,
Waving at birds, as carefree child.
The mailman slips, and down he goes,
In my grand seat, I laugh and pose.

So here I sit, a front-row seat,
With laughter echoing through the street.
Life unfolds like a funny play,
Outside my window, every day.

Frames of Distant Dreams

Painted skies in a world of dreams,
Each canvas holds hilarious schemes.
A squirrel disputes with a garden gnome,
Who knew my backyard could feel like home?

Children giggle, with ice cream smiles,
While moms make faces, yet walk in style.
The wind carries whispers of silly talk,
As daisies dance along the sidewalk.

Each frame I witness brings joy anew,
Like a sitcom set in sunlit hue.
The antics of life just steal the show,
From my little nook where the breezes blow.

So here I frame the joy I find,
In the fleeting moments that twist and bind.
Reality, a comedy so bright,
Through these windows, it feels just right.

Open Panes, Open Minds

Windows wide, let the laughter in,
Where quirky things sprout and spin.
A noodle race down the kitchen floor,
As kids declare it's what they adore.

A sock puppet gives a savvy speech,
While jellybeans blush in bright peach.
The world outside hums a silly tune,
As I sip lemonade beneath the moon.

The mail truck dances down the lane,
Like clumsy ballerinas on a train.
Every glance reveals a funny world,
With sights and sounds just whisked and twirled.

Let's open our hearts, our minds set free,
To embrace the joy of absurdity.
In this comedy of life, let's play,
With windows wide, let giggles stay.

A Glimpse of Tomorrow

Tomorrow whispers from across the street,
A dog starts jogging, on tiny feet.
A lady in pink jogs without a care,
With a feather boa billowing in the air.

A robot mowing with sleek finesse,
While neighbors stare, unable to guess.
Will we all join in this wild parade,
To laugh at the future we've all made?

I peek ahead, and what do I see?
A world where squirrels sip organic tea.
Dance parties hosted by ants in line,
In a quirky future that's simply divine.

So let's embrace what lies ahead,
With laughter echoing as our thread.
Tomorrow's glow is surely bright,
As I peer out, my heart feels light.

Perspectives Unseen

In a house perched high with windows wide,
A cat thinks it's a bird, while birds can't hide.
An old chair whispers tales of days gone by,
As socks slip off feet when laughter is nigh.

A painting winks, its humor sly,
While dust gathers secrets, oh me, oh my!
What a spectacle of life there's to be,
As the couch takes bets on who spills their tea!

Tapestry of Seasons

The curtains flutter like butterflies bold,
While winter shivers beneath a blanket of gold.
Spring brings a sneeze, and summer, a tan,
But fall leaves the room—nobody knows why it ran.

From cozy corners, whispers get tossed,
And plants give side-eyes to pots that are lost.
A clock ticks its jokes, time plays the fool,
While the broom dreams of tours at a cleaning school!

The Nature of Sight

Through a glass so clear, we spy on the fun,
As neighbors compete in who can bake a bun.
A dog gives a bark, the cat rolls its eyes,
While I sip my coffee, pretending to be wise.

A wall clock giggles as hands go around,
Counting all the antics and antics profound.
Here's to the laughter that leaps through the air,
In a theater of life, with no one to care!

Inward Journeys

I sat in my chair, a throne made of fluff,
Musing on life while pretending to bluff.
The mirror reflected a face full of dreams,
While my belly conspired with ice cream schemes.

To travel within, oh, what a delight!
A couch can be magic when the mood is right.
Exploring the realms of my snacks and my woes,
In this inward abyss, no one really knows!

Outward Glances

From the window I watch a squirrel with grace,
As it buries its stash in the neighbor's lace.
A mailman jogs by with a look of surprise,
While I pretend to check my own shoelace ties.

With popcorn in hand, I'm the audience here,
As life's grand performance fills me with cheer.
Let me be the critic, with a laugh and a sigh,
Giving stars to the antics that flutter by!

A Fractured Horizon

In a dwelling perched high, birds talk,
Gossiping tales as they squawk.
The cat on the sill rolls its eyes,
Dreaming of fishy surprise.

Sunset paints the walls with cheer,
While socks vanish, it's quite clear.
A sock thief's party, who would've thought?
Nowhere else can chaos be caught.

Neighbors wonder what's the deal,
Peeking through blinds, oh, what a reel!
Laughter erupts, a comedic note,
As I juggle snacks, trying not to gloat.

So here I sit, in this blissful mess,
Terracotta dreams in a vibrant dress.
With each glance outside, the world seems grand,
Just a little less tidy, but perfectly planned.

Colorful Unraveling

From the window, colors collide,
As squirrels plan their culinary ride.
A circus of chaos in bright display,
Hop on board, come what may!

The washing line whirls like a dance,
Under the sun, fabrics prance.
With a sock here and a shirt there,
What a delightful and crazy affair!

Birds sing in harmony, or is it a fight?
While cars honk, adding to the plight.
A parade of mishaps, all in fun,
What a splendid way to get things done!

Through this colorful lens, life takes flight,
Finding joy in simple delight.
With giggles and chuckles, I gaze outside,
Wishing every day would be this wild ride.

Visions of the Unfamiliar

Behind the glass, the world is a show,
With random acts of folly and woe.
A dog in a tutu leads the way,
While llamas audition for the next play.

Bicycles parade with more flair than grace,
As I sip my tea, chuckling at the race.
Here, every moment's a laugh in disguise,
With quirkiness written in the skies.

People waltz by with their heads held high,
In a world where umbrellas fly.
Each glance outside feeds my whimsy soul,
Caught in the joy of nonsensical roll.

Oh, my hilarious little corner, I say,
Where oddities bloom with no need to stray.
In this peculiar spectacle, I find my muse,
In visions of laughter, I'll never refuse.

The Canvas of Beyond

A canvas sprawled beyond the pane,
Where colors mix like joy and pain.
The neighbors shout, "Is it cake or art?"
As I ponder life, twirling a part.

Crafters outside with wild intent,
Create the most beautiful accident.
With glitter storms and laughter loud,
Oh, my quirky plaid-clad crowd!

A baker in a bizarre costume prances,
While the mailman does the cha-cha dances.
In my prized view, they spin and twirl,
Turning mundane life into a swirl.

From my little nook of ironic delight,
I relish in smiles, what a funny sight!
This canvas stretches wide and beyond,
A masterpiece of laughter, of which I'm so fond.

Perspectives from the Perch

From my high spot, I see it all,
Neighbors stumble, cats take a fall.
Birds gossip up on the power line,
While I sip tea and feel quite divine.

Peeking through curtains with little care,
I spy on the world - who will dare?
A dog in a tutu, quite a sight,
Makes me laugh 'til my tea takes flight.

A breeze flirts with my flimsy dress,
As I watch a squirrel in all its mess.
It scrambles and scampers, a sight to behold,
Nature's own circus, brave and bold.

In this kingdom of laughs, I reign supreme,
Watching life dance like a wild dream.
Each scene a play, each sound a cheer,
From my perch above, everything's clear.

Fathomless Sights Beyond

With a glance from my window, what do I spy?
An octogenarian rollerblading by.
With knee pads and care, he rolls like a pro,
As onlookers giggle, in awe - and whoa!

Traffic jams turn into baffling art,
As pigeons have council, discussing their part.
Twenty-five crows, all in a debate,
Deciding the best place to congregate.

Lovers exchange awkward, sidelong glances,
While a toddler in jeers leads wild dances.
I laugh at the chaos unfolding below,
Fathomless sights, my own comedy show.

In this world so bizarre, I'm content and bright,
Savoring moments, colorful light.
Gravity's pull seems to make one laugh,
Life's absurdity, a wobbly path.

Unfolding Life Beyond Pane

Through the glass, what a circus I find,
An elderly man, quite unconfined.
He's hula-hooping with ease and grace,
While I can't help but laugh at this pace.

A little girl leaps, pure joy in her spin,
While her dad's chasing after, wearing a grin.
The garbage truck's rumbling, making a scene,
As the raccoons decide it's their time to glean.

With every sunset, the chaos unfurls,
My neighbor's cat attempts to catch swirls.
Of butterflies flitting, too crafty, too quick,
As the cat just wobbles, then tries to stick.

In this hub of delight, I frolic with glee,
The jokes that life tells are just for me.
Each moment unfolds like a fresh, funny tale,
Through the pane of my life, I cannot fail.

Gazing into the Blue

Peering out into the vast blue skies,
I marvel at clouds doing wild flybys.
One looks like a whale, another a shoe,
Who knew the heavens hosted a zoo?

Laughter erupts as two kids on a bike,
Wobble and rattle, to avoid a spike.
Their giggles blend with the chirping of trees,
While ducks plotting mischief swim with ease.

Oh, a kite goes soaring, then dives like a ray,
Almost grazing a dog's big fluffy mane today.
Its owner shouts, "No! That's not a snack!"
As the dog leaps up, and the kite pulls back.

In each silly twist, in each chuckle we hear,
Life's painted in humor, let's give a cheer!
Gazing into the blue, I chuckle anew,
This world is a comedy, and laughter's the cue.

The Beyond Within

In a space where dreamers dwell,
And thoughts like bouncing balls do swell.
A window's frame with comic flair,
Peeks at the world without a care.

Curtains dance like wily ghosts,
While sunlight plays with shadowy hosts.
The furniture joins in the fun,
As chairs and tables try to run!

Laughter echoes through the air,
As mismatched socks begin to pair.
A sock puppet war breaks out anew,
In this quirky space for me and you.

With each bright angle, pranks ensue,
Even the dust bunnies join the crew.
In the cozy chaos, joy is found,
In every corner, laughter's sound.

Architecture of Aspiration

Sketches flutter in the breeze,
Like paper planes that tease and please.
Blueprints come alive at night,
As dreams construct with pure delight.

A ceiling fan spins tales so grand,
Of castles built from grains of sand.
Walls hum a tune, a silly jive,
Where hope and humor come alive.

Windows wink with a cheeky spark,
As squirrels outside play hide and hark.
Aboard this ship of foolish dreams,
Reality's not quite what it seems.

The sofa sports a hat and tie,
As cushions plot to reach the sky.
With every footstep, joy ignites,
In this wild concert of quirky sights.

Enchanted by the Horizon

A view so wide, it makes me grin,
Where eagles dare and dreams begin.
Clouds wander with a goofy pace,
As sunshine sprinkles laughter's trace.

Mountains wear their craggy frowns,
While valleys sport their cozy gowns.
The sun, a jester in the sky,
Waves at the stars as they float by.

Each hill tells jokes both old and new,
As daisies giggle in morning dew.
The horizon flirts, a playful tease,
Inviting all to laugh with ease.

With every dip and rise, we soar,
In blissful chaos, we explore.
The world a stage, absurd and bright,
In this grand play of day and night.

Nature's Kaleidoscope

Leaves rustle like a giggling crowd,
While squirrels scurry, silly and loud.
Petals twirl in a breezy dance,
Nature's jesters in vibrant pants.

The creek babbles like a cheeky sage,
Sharing secrets of every age.
Sunflowers bow with mighty grace,
While daisies prance in this open space.

A butterfly flutters, wearing a grin,
A tiny parade, where smiles begin.
The trees lean in to catch a laugh,
In this green world, we find our path.

Nature's joke is the best of all,
Where whimsy reigns, and worries fall.
In this grand tapestry, wild and bright,
Life's a jest, a pure delight.

An Invitation to Infinity

A door creaks wide, and what do I see?
A garden of wonders, where I sip my tea.
Butterflies dance, they tease and they play,
Inviting me closer, come join the ballet.

I trip on a pot, oh, what a surprise!
A flower peeks up with little round eyes.
It whispers to me, 'Let's plot a great scheme,
To float like a cloud, or swim in a dream.'

The sun paints the walls with a yellowy hue,
Squirrels are planning their own little coup.
They chatter and giggle, oh what a sight!
While I sit and wonder, 'Is this all delight?'

In this whimsical space, where the laughter is free,
I'm queen of the jesters and fit for a spree.
So send in the clowns, let the fun never cease,
An invitation to joy, to the heart and the peace.

Eyes on the Edge of Being

Peering outside with a curious grin,
A cat on the windowsill, ready to in.
It ponders the pigeons, plotting a snack,
While I'm stuck dreaming of all the things I lack.

Sunbeams come tumbling, a warm, lazy light,
Where shadows can frolic, they dance in delight.
A mop in my hand, I'm named the great sage,
While mop 'n' the floor starts to center the stage.

A snail slides by with a shell on its back,
It laughs at my chaos, 'What's with the clock?'
I nod at the scene, feeling quite the fool,
As the garden throws confetti, I'm lost in my drool.

Yet from this small window, my heart takes a leap,
Into the absurdity, the giggles I keep.
What if life's nonsense is all that I need?
Adventure awaits with the silliest creed!

Breath of the Open Air

Outside the breeze whispers tales of the day,
While I peak out cautiously, come what may.
A ruckus of laughter invades my still space,
A parade of odd figures, each with a face.

The hedgehog and rabbit are forming a band,
With carrots and acorns, they're giving a hand.
They strum on the herbs, and they sing with delight,
While I'm chuckling softly, oh what a sight!

A butterfly lands on my shoe with a wink,
It leans in real close, 'Shall we dance or just blink?'
I giggle and ponder, what could it mean?
Perhaps life is just one big whimsical scene.

And so in the chaos, I breathe in the air,
With laughter abound, I could never despair.
Though I'm just a spectator, it's clear as can be,
In this mad little world, it's the glee that sets me free.

A Lens on Life's Poetry

I open my window to a marvelous show,
As squirrels recite lines, as silly as dough.
I take out my pen, ready to jot,
The poetry written by critters and pot.

The grass sings a tune, a hip-hoppy beat,
While ants march in rhythm, oh what a feat!
With giggles and pitter-patters at play,
Nature's grand jesters are brightening my day.

A frog in the pond croaks deep with great flair,
Fitness regime, bouncing, without any care.
They leap and they land with a plop and a splash,
In this comedy act, they make quite the bash.

So here at my desk with a chuckle or two,
I laugh at the simple, the odd, and the true.
With a lens on this life, there's much to relate,
In the poetry written by nature—first-rate!

Ribbons of Air and Light

In a space where the sunlight plays,
The dust bunnies dance in their jolly ways.
Each beam is a ribbon, a playful plight,
While shadows giggle at the edge of night.

Chairs creak and squeak, like old comic strips,
A parade of socks, each with silly grips.
The view is a circus of hubbub and cheer,
Where the plants do the conga, oh dear, oh dear!

Windows wide open, the breeze takes a leap,
Tickling the curtains, making them weep.
Birds wear top hats and dance across the skies,
A raucous affair, oh how time flies!

With laughter that echoes, the sunset declines,
The laughter lingers like old, happy vines.
In this room of whimsy, with joy, we imbue,
Ribbons of air, shining bright and askew.

Glimpses of Grace

Peeking through panes with a curious glee,
I spot a parade of squirrels, fancy-free.
They jest and they frolic, they climb and they play,
As if rehearsing for a grand cabaret!

Oh look at that couple, they're tangled in vines,
Maybe they're practicing new dance lines?
Their laughter erupts like a fizzy soft drink,
In this gallery of life, it's hip to be pink!

Drapes flutter gently, whispering jokes,
While chairs tell me tales of ancestral folks.
Each crack in the wall has a story to tell,
Of mishaps and giggles, it rings like a bell!

Amidst all the chaos, a calmness sets in,
This little slice of funk is where fun begins.
With glimpses of grace, through the puzzling view,
Life struts its stuff in a frolic of hue.

Beyond Faded Curtains

Beyond the curtains, the world goes amok,
A cat claims the couch like a prized old clock.
Tap dancing in slippers, it's quite the charade,
While cushions are tossed in a soft, fluffy parade!

The clock's tick-tock joins in the playful affair,
Counting the chuckles and stories we share.
Echoes of laughter bounce off the walls,
In a whirl of glee, the mischief enthralls!

Plants sprout invitations of 'come join the fun,'
While sunbeams conspire to shine everyone.
In this tapestry woven with giggles and sighs,
Life's silly antics hover beneath the skies.

With a wiggle and waggle, the day drifts away,
Leaving behind stories that endlessly play.
Beyond faded curtains, the magic will brew,
In this playful domain, life's a comedic view.

Secrets Held in Sunbeams

In sunbeams that whisper, secrets are spun,
Tickling the atmosphere, oh what a run!
A spider's web sparkles in morning's embrace,
While dust motes dance like they're in outer space.

The clock gives a wink, it's time for a laugh,
Mixing up moments like a silly old chaff.
With shadows who join in the game and the jest,
Mirth piles up high, never letting you rest!

Through windows ajar, a parade echoes near,
Bouncing off walls, spreading joy and good cheer.
Each ray of sunshine holds giggles galore,
A concert of whimsy, impossible to ignore!

So come take a peek at the silliness spun,
In the secrets held tightly by laughter and fun.
A marvelous place where joy is the glue,
And the world is a stage seen from each view.

A Place Where Thoughts Wander

In a space where laughter blooms,
I sat between teacups and brooms.
The cat wore shades, quite the charmer,
Sipping water, posing like a farmer.

A sock on the wall, a hat on the chair,
Spinning stories from thin air.
While the ceiling fans whisper in jest,
I ponder the clouds, put my thoughts to rest.

The plants gossip, oh what a show!
One claimed it knew the way to go.
With echoes of mischief on the breeze,
I conjured up dreams with utmost ease.

Here, woes take a vacation, quite grand,
Where the world outside is perfectly planned.
With antics aplenty, spirits fly,
In this whimsical den, oh me, oh my!

Echoes of the Exterior

The window swings wide, what a delight,
Catching whispers from day into night.
With squirrels organizing acorn fights,
And birds rehearsing their million flights.

A dog barks loudly, a cat strikes back,
In a comedy sketch, they stage an attack.
While rain tap dances upon the ground,
I sip my tea, enjoying the sound.

The neighbors argue over what's for dinner,
I chuckle softly, a silent winner.
With a glimpse of their world, I can't help but beam,
Their dramas and traumas blend into a dream.

As laughter bounces from old bricks and beams,
I find joy in the cracks, in the seams.
The echoes of life, a curious play,
Here in my vantage, I laugh all day!

Vistas of the Soul

On the ledge, with an eager view,
I saw my thoughts bounce, dance, and skew.
From golden rays to clouds all grey,
My soul's canvas colors the day.

A breeze came in, with tickles and tease,
The curtains swayed, and with such ease,
I spun in circles, dizzy with glee,
While the mug told tales of caffeine and me.

Reflections of wonder, like bubbles they rise,
Curious faces beneath those bright skies.
My heart skips notes in this playful whirl,
With giggles and dreams, my thoughts unfurl.

In this vibrant nook, creativity flows,
Whispering secrets that nobody knows.
Dancing shadows paint stories anew,
In this vibrant space, my spirit just flew!

Beyond Boundaries of Walls

With paper walls and ceiling high,
I plotted a course, just me and the sky.
A map made of scribbles, so clever and neat,
Leading to lands with candy to eat.

The carpet's a river, the chair is a boat,
Setting sail on a whimsical float.
I laughed with the cushions, joined their spree,
While the clock ticked on, sipping cherry tea.

Outside, the folks hurry, but here I glide,
Where silly thoughts and dreams collide.
Such treasures hidden in each little crack,
With giggles and joy, there's no looking back.

In this playground of whimsy, delightfully spun,
Life rushes past, yet here we have fun.
Beyond these four walls, I've built a realm,
Where laughter and chaos are at the helm!

A Kaleidoscope of Vistas

From a box of strange delights,
I see a cat in silly tights.
A bird that dances, spins, and twirls,
While squirrels juggle acorns, give it a whirl!

Colors pop and twist around,
As laughter echoes, joy is found.
With every glance, a new surprise,
Even the goldfish rolled its eyes!

The neighbor waves with mismatched socks,
While I pretend to guard my box.
It's like the world's a carnival scene,
Where even my plants have turned to green!

A peek outside, what do I see?
A dancing broom, just like in tea!
Oh, the wonders from this odd perch,
Life feels like quite the playful search!

Reflections on the Edge

Peering out, I see a cake,
A birthday surprise, for goodness' sake!
But it's not for me, oh what a bummer,
As the frosting sings a sugary summer.

The window frames a balmy day,
Where penguins parade in a funny ballet.
They slip and slide with rhymes so sweet,
As I sip tea, chuckling in my seat.

A moose on roller skates whizzes by,
Waving a pizza, oh my, oh my!
Adventures unfold just outside my door,
Where socks go missing and make me roar!

So here I sit, with a chuckle or two,
The world is a stage, oh so askew.
With every glance, a grin returns,
In this playful realm, laughter burns!

Lattice of Light and Shadow

Through the glass, shadows play,
A silly cat on a bright buffet.
Twirling napkins, a dance so odd,
While a sock puppet gives a nod.

Light spills in with glittering beams,
Tickling my nose, igniting dreams.
Where car tires recite comic tales,
And my laughter rides on the bus trails.

A butterfly lands, sips my drink,
I offer it cake, sees it blink.
A parade of ants march in sync,
In this pop-up show, no time to think!

So here I lounge, bask in delight,
While outside chaos takes flight.
In this lattice of fun and grace,
Who knew silliness could find its place?

Beyond the Sill

Beyond the sill, what do I find?
A troupe of frogs in a conga line.
With tiny hats and shoes that squeak,
They frolic around, it's quite the week!

A rabbit juggles carrots with ease,
While bees hum a tune in the breeze.
A snail races by with quite the flair,
In this world outside, who needs despair?

Each glance reveals a wacky delight,
Where even the trees are dressed just right.
With faces carved in bark of old,
They whisper stories, oh so bold!

So here I sit, a smile I'll grow,
At the quirky show put on by nature's flow.
The view is grand, with laughter it thrills,
Life's silly dance, beyond the sills!

Landscapes of Reflection

I peeped from my window, what a sight,
A garden gnome giving a cat a fright.
Birds in a choir, with a tune so sweet,
While squirrels debate on the nuts they'll eat.

A dog in a top hat waltzes around,
While ducks in a pond hold a court with a sound.
Lawn chairs are gossiping, oh what a fuss,
As I sip my tea, I feel quite the plus.

The sun takes a bow, the stars give a cheer,
My little view's filled with laughter and beer.
Oh, life from my window's a whimsical play,
And I join the fun from my seat every day.

Dreamscapes Behind Glass

Behind my clear glass, the world wears a grin,
As a squirrel's nut party breaks out with a spin.
The flowers are dancing, their petals a-flutter,
While bees in tuxedos discuss all the butter.

Clouds drift like marshmallows, fluffy and sweet,
While rainbows engage in a colorful feat.
This madcap tableau, a grand spectacle shown,
As the sun steals the show, through the glass it has grown.

I chuckle and wave at the antics in view,
My windows a portal to nonsense anew.
In laughter, I bask in this whimsical game,
As the world goes all silly, I giggle the same.

From the Lofty Ledge

From my lofty perch, I survey the land,
Where frogs wear sunglasses and each holds a band.
The trees are all dressed in their finest of green,
As branches do the cha-cha, a sight to be seen.

Fashioned ants hold a parade down the lane,
In miniature floats, they dance in the rain.
The breeze delivers jokes from the birds in flight,
While turtles mud-wrestle, what a curious sight!

Oh, laughter erupts from my higher up seat,
Where clouds whisper secrets of joy, oh so sweet.
In my snug little nook, all the whimsy unfolds,
As the charm of this world never gets old.

The Air Between Us

In this cozy space, hilarity reigns,
With laughter that bubbles like summer-time rains.
A cat on the windowsill keeps up a chat,
With birds doing stand-up, a comical spat.

I toss back my head, the giggles set free,
At a leap frog concert, so wild and so free.
A dog in a wig plays the tambourine loud,
While I cheer with glee, feeling utterly proud.

As the world spins around like a playful kite,
Every joke and each quip brings warmth and delight.
In this wonderful air, the comedy flares,
Keeping spirits so high, in these humorous layers.

Uncharted Skies Await

In a chair by the window, I dream a little,
Birds fly past, making me chuckle and giggle.
Thoughts of adventures just outside my pane,
But here I sit, sipping tea and feeling vain.

The clouds seem to whisper, 'Come out and play!'
While I ponder why Mondays always delay.
Sunshine's a tease, through curtains it peeps,
Yet I sink deeper, lost in my heaps.

A squirrel steps by, with a look on his face,
Like he has secret plans to leave this space.
But here I am, munching on snacks galore,
As the world rushes past, outside my door.

So I wave to the sky with a sprinkle of glee,
Wondering if one day, it will finally see,
That I, the great dreamer, can roam everywhere,
Yet still find the fun in my cozy old chair.

Silent Observations

Peeking through glasses, I watch the parade,
Of neighbors on sidewalks, and pets unafraid.
One dog in a tutu, what's this fashion craze?
While I sip my coffee, a delight for days.

There's drama unfolding in yard by yard,
With kids on their scooters, playing hard.
A cat plots revenge from atop a tall fence,
While I wonder if life is truly this dense.

Moments collide in a splendid ballet,
Each giggle and shout carrying me away.
Yet I remain fixed in this soft, cushy nest,
Counting the oddities, feeling quite blessed.

So I note down the laughter, the tears that will fall,
From this prime observation post, I see it all.
And a smile creeps in as the day's stories weave,
Silent yet loud, in what I believe.

The Portal to the Unseen

Here in my quarter of comfort and fluff,
I ponder if outside is really that rough.
Adventures await beyond the front gate,
But it's cozy in here, so I tackle my fate.

Outside it's a circus, with chaos and light,
While I munch my popcorn, it's a comical sight.
Footsteps on sidewalks, laughter in the breeze,
Oh, to be out there, but the couch said, 'Please!'

The world spins around with a jingle and sway,
Yet here on my throne, I'm queen for the day.
Through this portal I watch, with a grin oh so wide,
At the hilarious antics of life outside.

So I'll chuckle and smile from my own little nook,
While the world frolics madly, I'll read my good book.
In this portal I gaze, oh what tales might unfold?
Yet right here I'll stay, feeling comfy and bold.

Broad Horizons of Dreaming

In the sunlit corner, my visions expand,
While the cat gives me looks like she doesn't understand.
My fantasies float like balloons in the air,
While reality waits, with an unkempt hair.

I've painted the skies with colors so bright,
As the clock ticks away, it's a curious sight.
Broad horizons shimmer, with dreams on the line,
Yet I'm here in my pajamas, just sipping on wine.

Each glance out the window, a giggle confides,
At the world's crazy hustle and bustling rides.
A splash of absurdity colors the day,
While I sit in my bubble, all silly and sway.

With each shift of my gaze, new wonders I find,
In this cheerful invention, I've crafted my mind.
So let them rush out, in their serious swarm,
I'll stay nestled here, in my daydreams so warm.

Beyond the Threshold of Light

In a room where curtains play,
A dance of sun, a bright ballet.
The dust bunnies frolic in warm rays,
While I ponder my laundry delays.

My neighbor's plants, they wave and cheer,
While I sip coffee, feeling sheer.
Their leafy gossip fills the air,
I try to focus, but who really cares?

With each new sound, a plot unfolds,
A tale of mischief, daring and bold.
The clock ticks slowly, oh what a plight,
Should I nap or just bask in light?

The outside world seems far away,
But inside here, it's a holiday.
So let them wonder, let them pry,
From my threshold, I'll just sigh!

Embracing the Faraway

The horizon calls, a tempting tease,
Yet here I sit, wrapped in freeze.
A donut box, my faithful friend,
This taste of joy, it'll never end.

I dream of travel, of sights to see,
But my couch insists it's where I should be.
With snacks piled high and shows to binge,
Adventure can wait, that's my cringe.

Through the window, kids fly kites,
While I debate my Friday nights.
Their laughter echoes, their spirits bright,
While I'm a hermit, holding tight.

One day I'll wander, that's my view,
But for now, I'll munch and enjoy my stew.
Because here within my cozy nest,
Life's faraway lands can wait for the best!

Whispered Secrets of the Skyline

Up above the world, a sight so grand,
I spy a squirrel that's got a plan.
He's plotting acorns, oh what a sight,
While I'm just here, stuck in my plight.

The skyline sparkles, a shimmering tease,
But my pizza's calling with greasy ease.
Oh to be graceful, like that bird in flight,
Instead, I'm a snack machine in the night.

With every honk, a new drama starts,
While I stay enclosed, nursing my tarts.
The city sings, it dances and thrives,
Meanwhile, I'm here, counting my fries.

The horizon stretches, a canvas so wide,
But these couch cushions, they're my pride.
So here I'll stay, in my comfy cocoon,
As the skyline whispers, I'll save it for noon.

Through the Veil of Glass

Peeking through this pane so bright,
I watch the world with pure delight.
People scurry, dogs chase tails,
I sip my tea, I've got no fails.

The sun reflects a golden fire,
While I recline with no need to aspire.
A pigeon struts, he's come to tease,
While I chuckle, feeling at ease.

With every car that zooms outside,
I'm content to let my worries slide.
Oh, to be young and adventurous too,
But I'd rather binge-watch and chew.

So let the clouds float, let the winds blow,
Through this pane, I have a front-row view.
No need for tickets or fancy flights,
My window world brings me pure delights!

The Great Expanse Undisturbed

In a place where no one peeks,
The curtains dance, a laugh it seeks.
A squirrel spies, with cheeky charm,
As I sip tea, safe from harm.

A cactus winks, its spines on show,
The cat observes, with head held low.
Outside the world, a circus ride,
While I just grin, trapped inside.

Birds gossip loud, they chirp and tease,
A parade of clouds, all eyes on me.
The goldfish swims, in silent glee,
This opulent throne is all for me!

I wave to friends on distant streets,
With every honk, my heart skips beats.
They think I'm mad, just sitting still,
But I'm the king, with endless thrill.

Windowsill Whispers

A plant with secrets, leaves that sway,
Whispering tales of the day.
It knows the gossip, the latest craze,
While I just grin, in my sunny haze.

The curtains flutter, a cheeky breeze,
As if to share the world's unease.
With every flap, they dance with glee,
Inflation? Who cares? Just tea for me!

The ants parade in perfect line,
While I giggle at their tiny design.
They've got the moves, those little guys,
While I stare out with laughing eyes.

Sunshine beams, the neighbors shout,
I'm here for laughs and not the doubt.
With every glance from my cozy nook,
I jot my tales in a little book.

The Outlook of Wonder

Peering out at the busy street,
Life's a show, such a comic feat.
A dog in boots, a cat in shades,
Oh what a sight, the laughter parades!

The mailman slips on a banana peel,
His grace is surely a surreal deal.
I chuckle soft, to keep it low,
And think of jokes I want to throw.

With neighbors bickering about their lawn,
It's a Netflix show, but live at dawn.
In my seat, I munch on snackies galore,
As the world outside opens its door.

Every moment, a comic gold,
Stories of life, both young and old.
I scribble down my silly muse,
In the great gallery of humorous views.

Frames of Enchantment

With frames that hold the world so tight,
I gaze upon the whimsical sight.
A parade of ants, in perfect dawdle,
While I sip juice from a fancy bottle.

A neighbor yells, 'Where's my shoe?'
As cats conspire, a subtle crew.
Like a play, I laugh and stare,
In my enchanted world, beyond compare.

Through the lens of mischief, I behold,
Stories of life, forever told.
From butterflies to a wayward kite,
Every glance makes my heart feel light.

With each new wink from the turning leaves,
This wonky view my spirit weaves.
In frames of jest, I'm never blue,
For life's sweet magic is all askew.

The Imagination's Outlook

A cat on a ledge, quite wise in her stance,
Pretends to inspect the great world by chance.
She spies on the squirrels, so fluffy and sly,
As they scurry around, she lets out a sigh.

The curtains are billowing, dancing with glee,
Whispering secrets, just between you and me.
A bird with a hat, it swoops in for a peek,
Causing all passersby to stop, wiggle, and squeak.

Dandelions tickle the windows so bright,
As the daft little gnome grins in pure delight.
He juggles the raindrops that slip from the glass,
While neighbors chuckle about the odd class.

In fantasies painted with laughter and cheer,
The view entertains, pulling all close and near.
So take a seat here and let your mind roam,
For laughter's the key to make any place home.

Starlight from the Windowsill

On the sill is a parrot who tells silly jokes,
While mist out the window makes thieves out of folks.
A star drops its glitter, a shimmy and shake,
Causing the cat to leap high, then ache.

The moon plays a tune on its harp made of cheese,
As shadows of mice scamper over with ease.
They're plotting a dance, oh what a grand sight,
Until clumsy old Freddie puts out their starlight.

A cactus in bloom sings the blues with a grin,
Impressing the passersby, oh what a din!
While neighbors in nightgowns gossip 'til dawn,
Sharing tales of the wild, the mischievous spawn.

In starlit mischief, the imagination flies,
Through laughter and folly, nobody cries.
For every window gleams with adventures anew,
Where the night is alive with nonsense in view.

Layers of Light and Shadow

Behind the old blinds lurks a Docker named Dave,
Awaiting the sunlight, so bold and so brave.
He dances in shadows, twirls with great flair,
Hoping the sunbeam will find him somewhere.

A potted geranium snores on the sill,
Holding dreams of grandeur and lightness at will.
She sways to the rhythm of heat on her leaves,
While debating with curtains if she'll take the eaves.

In the depth of the corners, a raccoon named Lou,
Dons shades made of cobwebs, declares, "Who are you?"

Just a patch of moonlight spills softly around,
As mischief and laughter mix sounds without sound.

A dance of delight through each layer displayed,
Where shadows and light play the clever charade.
With giggles and chuckles, the world winks and beams,
In the layers of whimsy, we stitch all our dreams.

Visionary Panoramas

From heights of my kingdom—a couch—a grand sweep,
I spy the odd couple that's terribly cheap.
On bicycles shiny, they race with a cheer,
Their helmets adorned with bright stickers unclear.

A clown in a tutu just waved from the park,
Jumping through puddles while leaving a spark.
With candy in hand and balloons up, up high,
He tiptoes past pigeons that giggle and fly.

A dog on a skateboard rolls by with a grin,
With sunglasses on, oh, what a bowl of win!
But splash! through the puddles, old Mr. McGee,
Gets soaked by a wave that's wild as can be.

In visions so quirky, the panorama's bright,
With laughter and chaos, oh what a delight!
So join in the folly, let spirits rejoice,
For each laugh we share brings a whimsical voice.

A Symphony of Distant Sounds

Sitting here with tea in hand,
I hear the chatter from the land.
Birds gossiping, trees have their say,
Life outside, in a comical display.

The dog next door barks a tune,
While squirrels dance 'neath the moon.
Each sound, a note in my ear,
A symphony of laughter, oh so dear.

Windows rattle with a tale or two,
As cars pass by, what a view!
Folk in hats, so grandly dressed,
Chasing their dreams, but not quite blessed.

With a snack in hand, I take it all in,
The beauty of chaos, where do I begin?
A world of quirks, each moment pure,
In this funny play, I find my cure.

In Search of Clarity

Peering out, I squint and stare,
The world outside, a jumbled affair.
Is that a cat or just a hat?
Who knew clarity could feel so flat?

Lawn chairs mingle with lazy bees,
While fence posts groan with stories, if you please.
What's that over there, a lopsided grin?
Ah, it's just the neighbor's new skin!

Glasses half-full with a splash of charm,
Yet wisdom slips like a untrained arm.
Each glance reveals something absurd,
Clarity smiles, but is quite disturbed.

Searching for peace through a haze of delight,
In this carnival, all feels just right.
With a chuckle, I choose to stay,
In this quirky scene, come what may!

Window to the World

My window frames a busy street,
Where pigeons strut with a comical beat.
A little girl jumps rope, takes a leap,
While folks trip over their own two feet!

Here's a man with one giant shoe,
Lost in thought, and I giggle too.
Across the way, a cat holds court,
With an air of grandeur, a feline sport.

People wave like they're in a play,
Got to love their quirky ballet.
Every glance outside is a sitcom scene,
I laugh so hard, I turn a bit green.

With tea in hand and a cozy spot,
This window shows me all I've got.
Life's a riot, who needs a view,
When hilarity stares back at you?

Horizons Beyond Glass

Looking out, the world feels bright,
Yet each moment gives me a fright.
A squirrel in a scarf, how absurdly chic,
While neighbors argue over who's meek.

A bird whistles in a tuneful haze,
I think it's singing about some grand craze.
Two old timers play checkers in style,
With a deck of cards, what's their guile?

The wind whispers secrets, oh so sly,
While I chuckle, watching time fly.
Everyone rushes, curiously daft,
In this delightful dance, I'm warmly laughed.

So I sit back and soak it in,
Life at the glass, where laughter begins.
Horizons sparkle with joy and sass,
In this funny play, time can't pass!